This 202__ Diary belongs to:

_____

_____

JANUARY

Week 1

Week 2

JANUARY

Week 3

Week 4

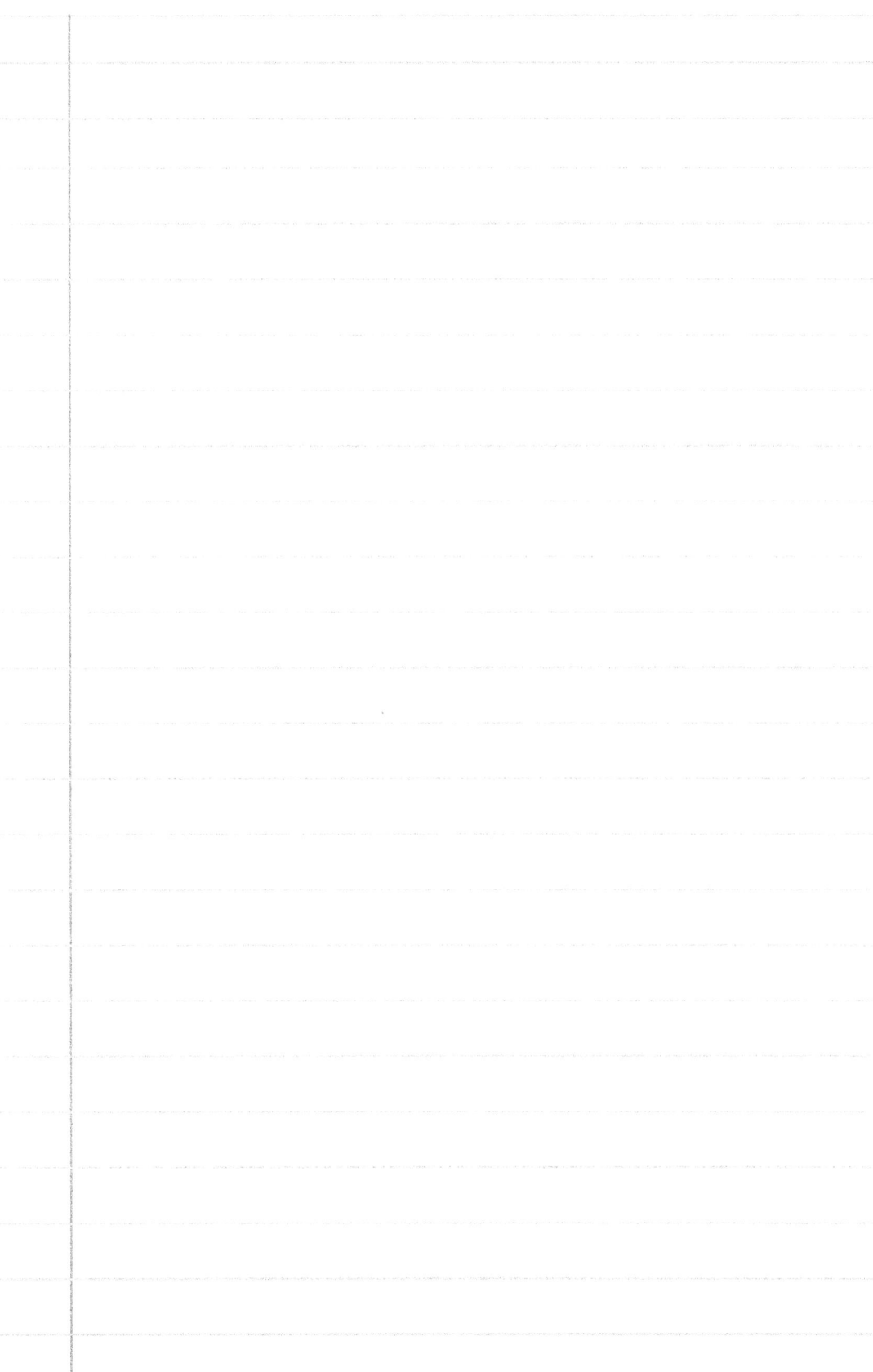

FEBRUARY

Week 1

Week 2

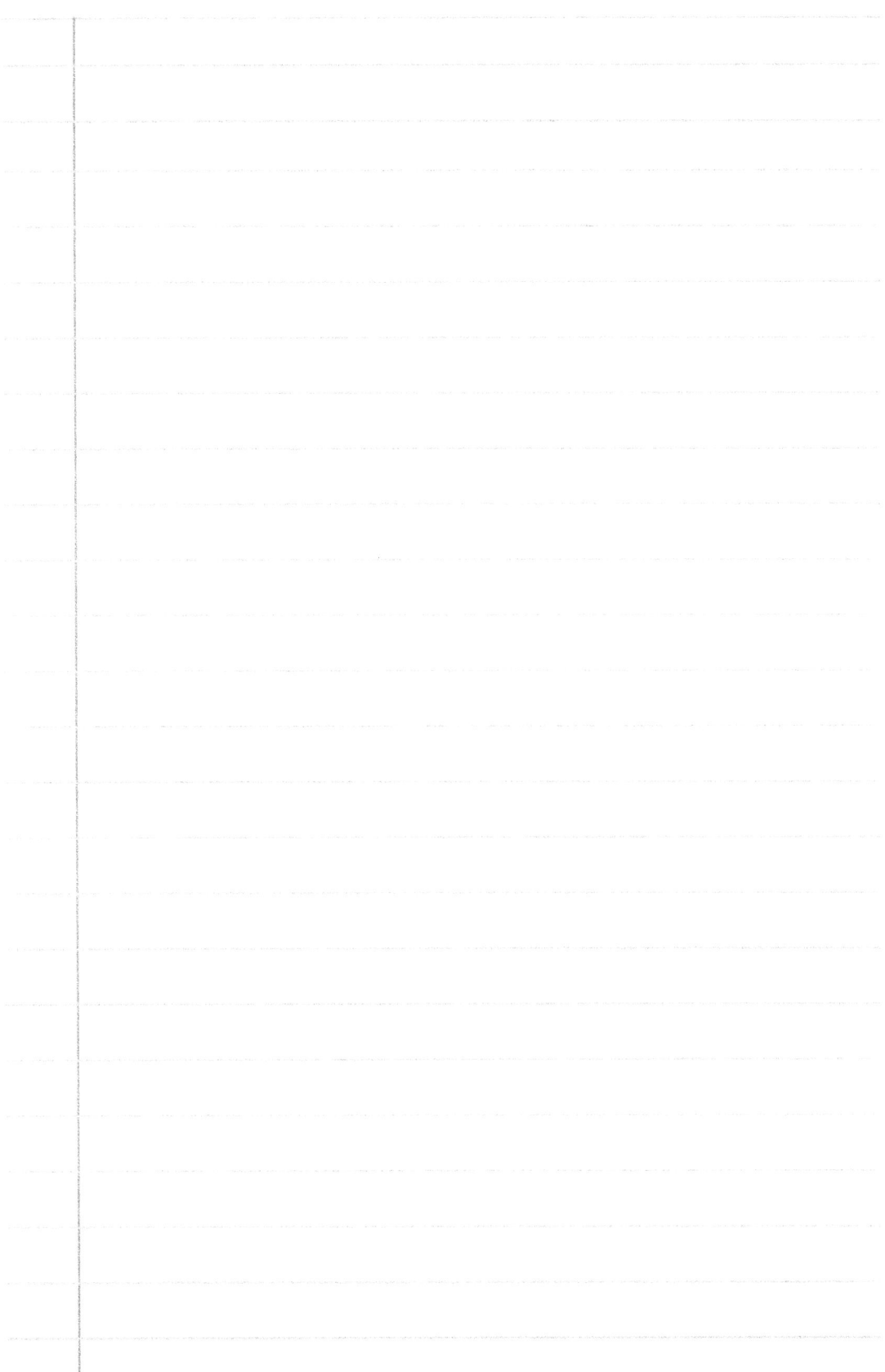

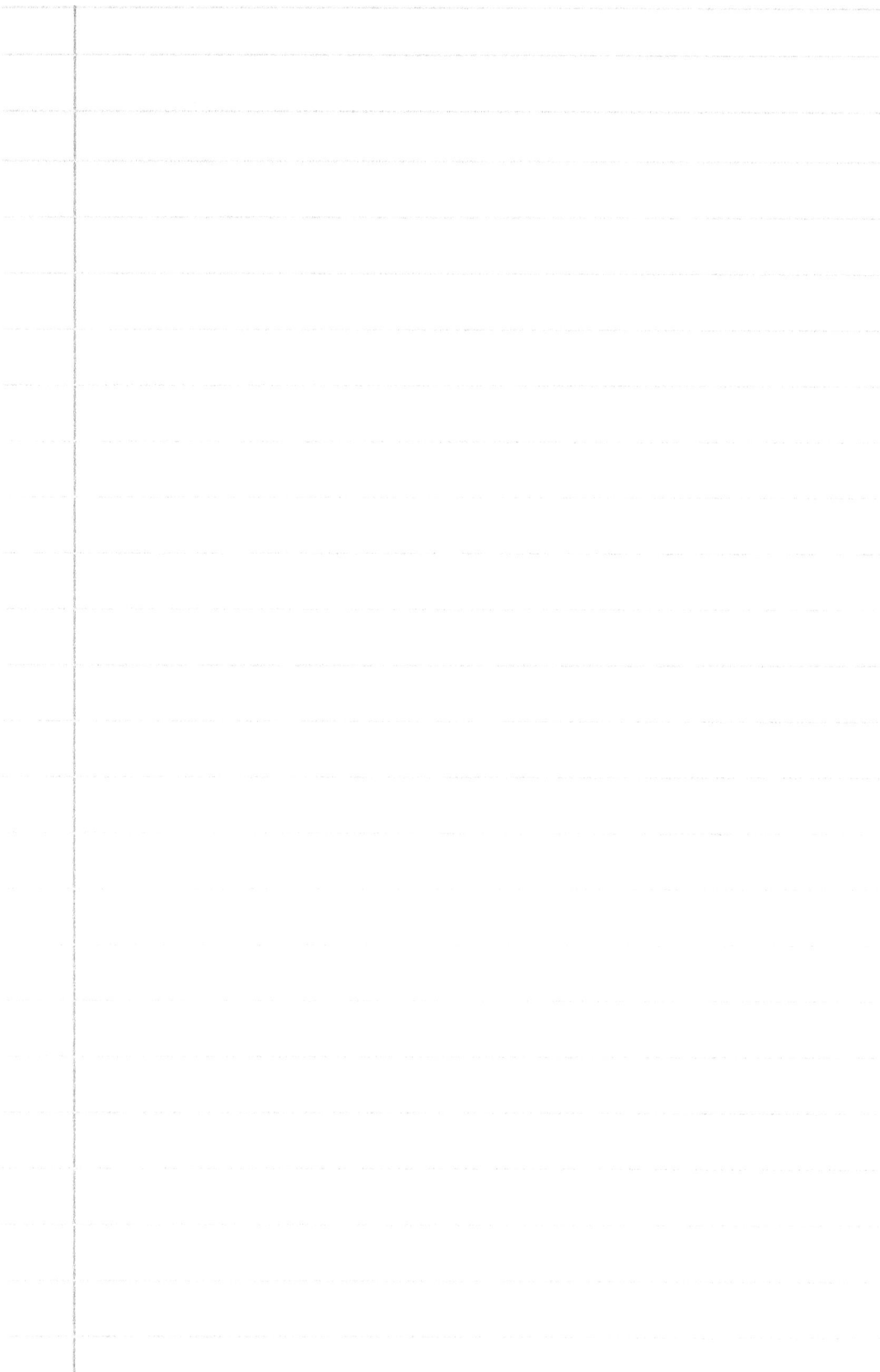

FEBRUARY

Week 3

Week 4

MARCH

Week 1

Week 2

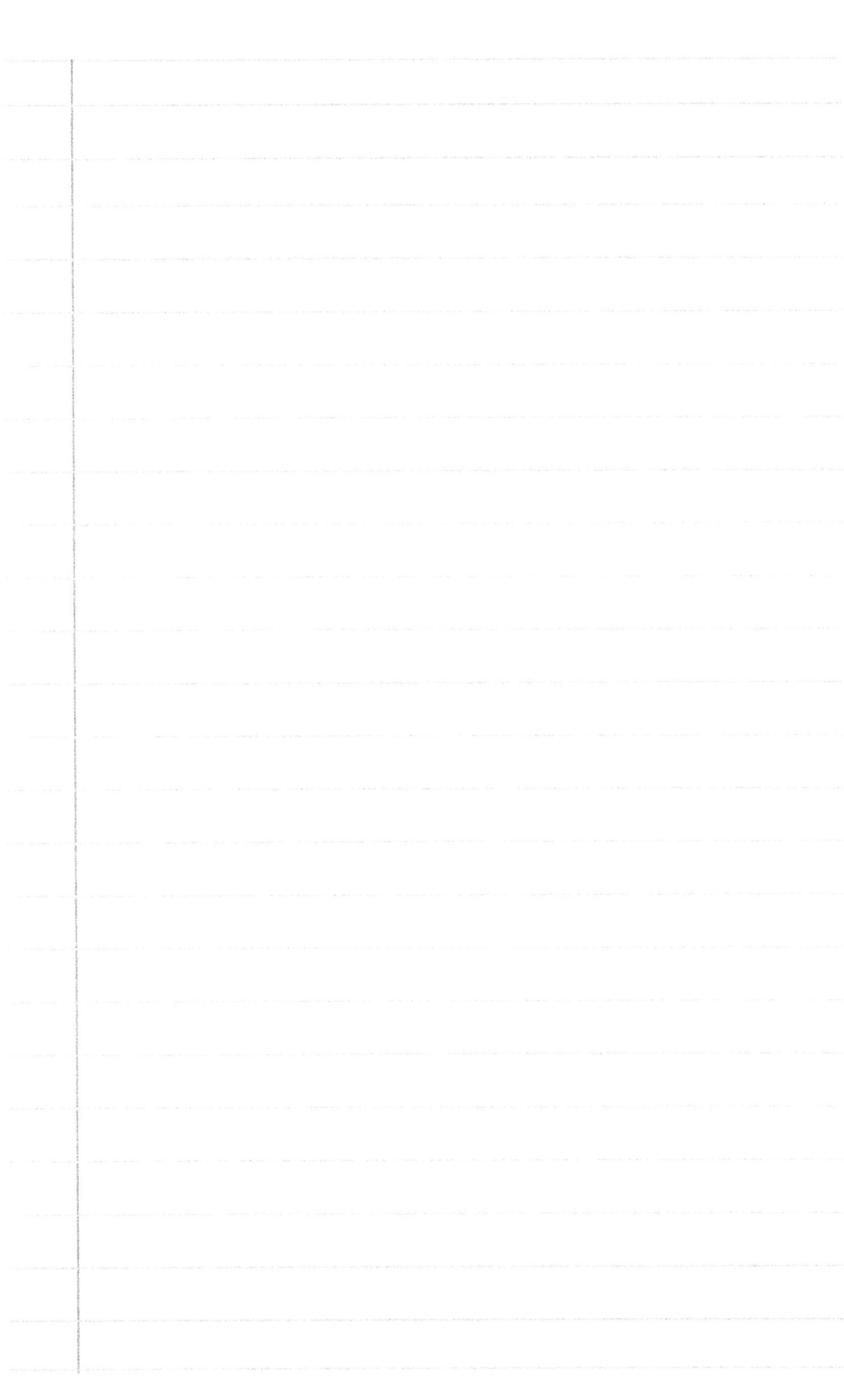

MARCH

Week 3

Week 4

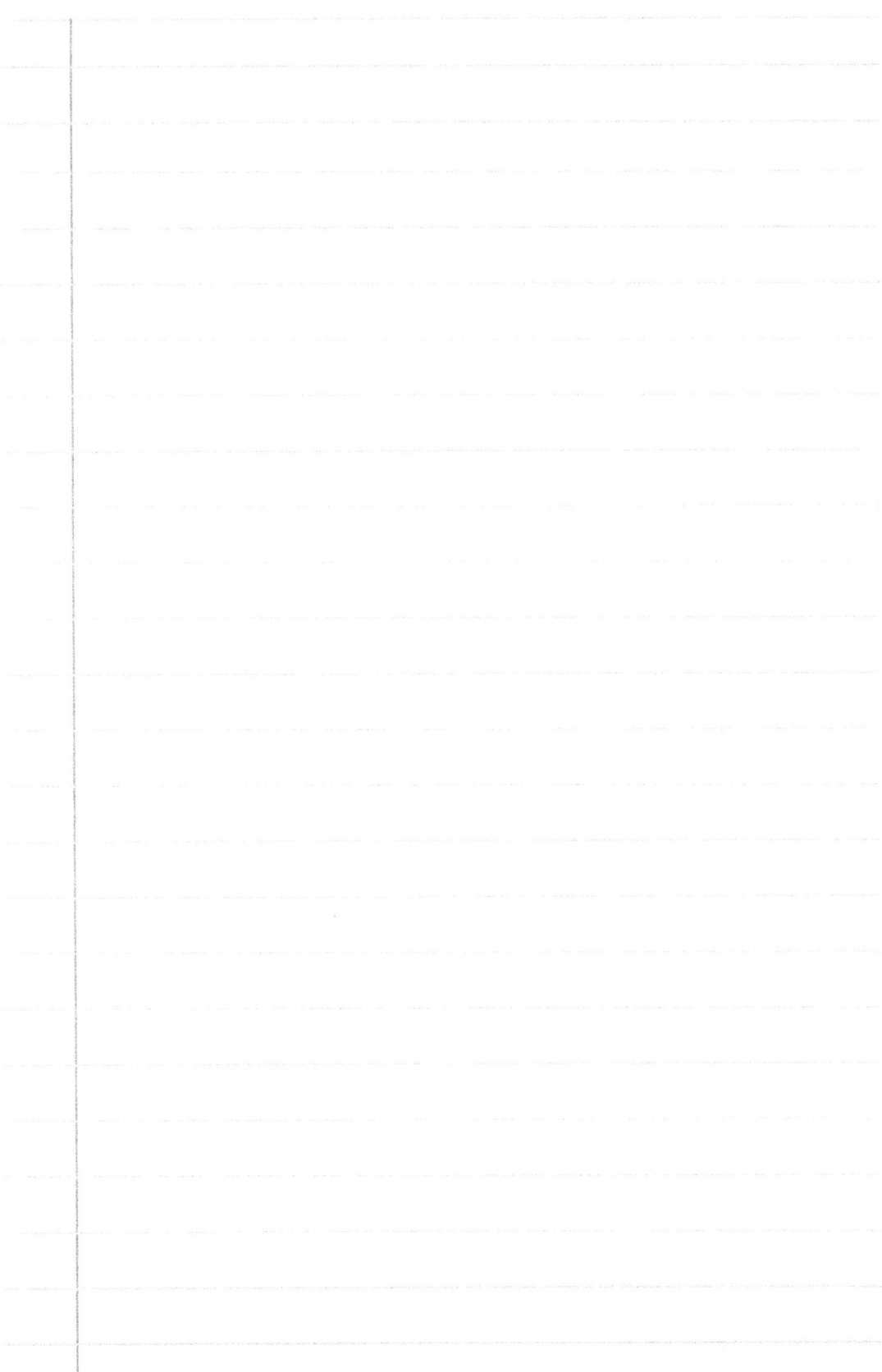

APRIL

Week 1

Week 2

APRIL

Week 3

Week 4

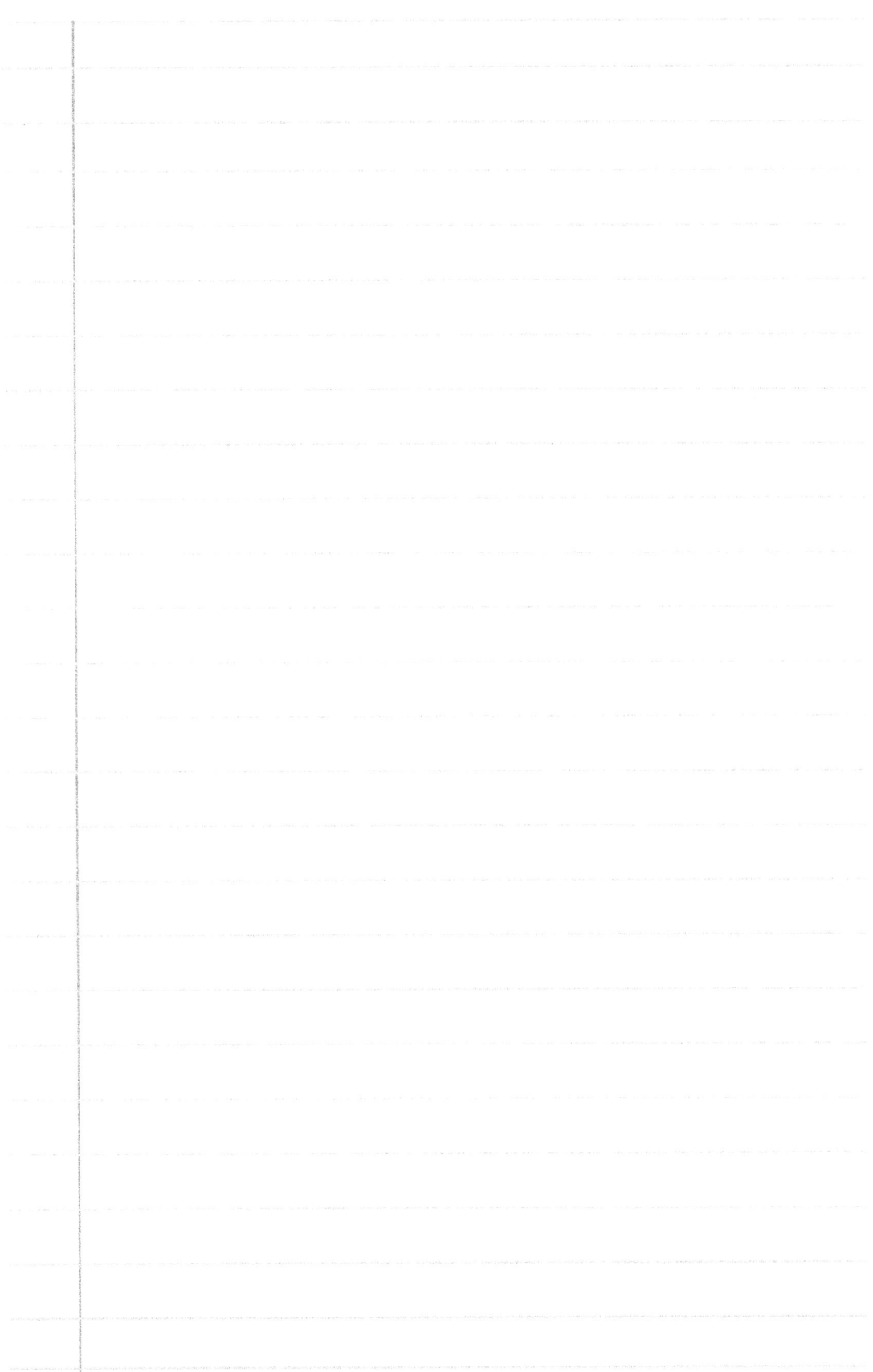

MAY

Week 1

Week 2

MAY

Week 3

Week 4

JUNE

Week 1

Week 2

JUNE

Week 3

Week 4

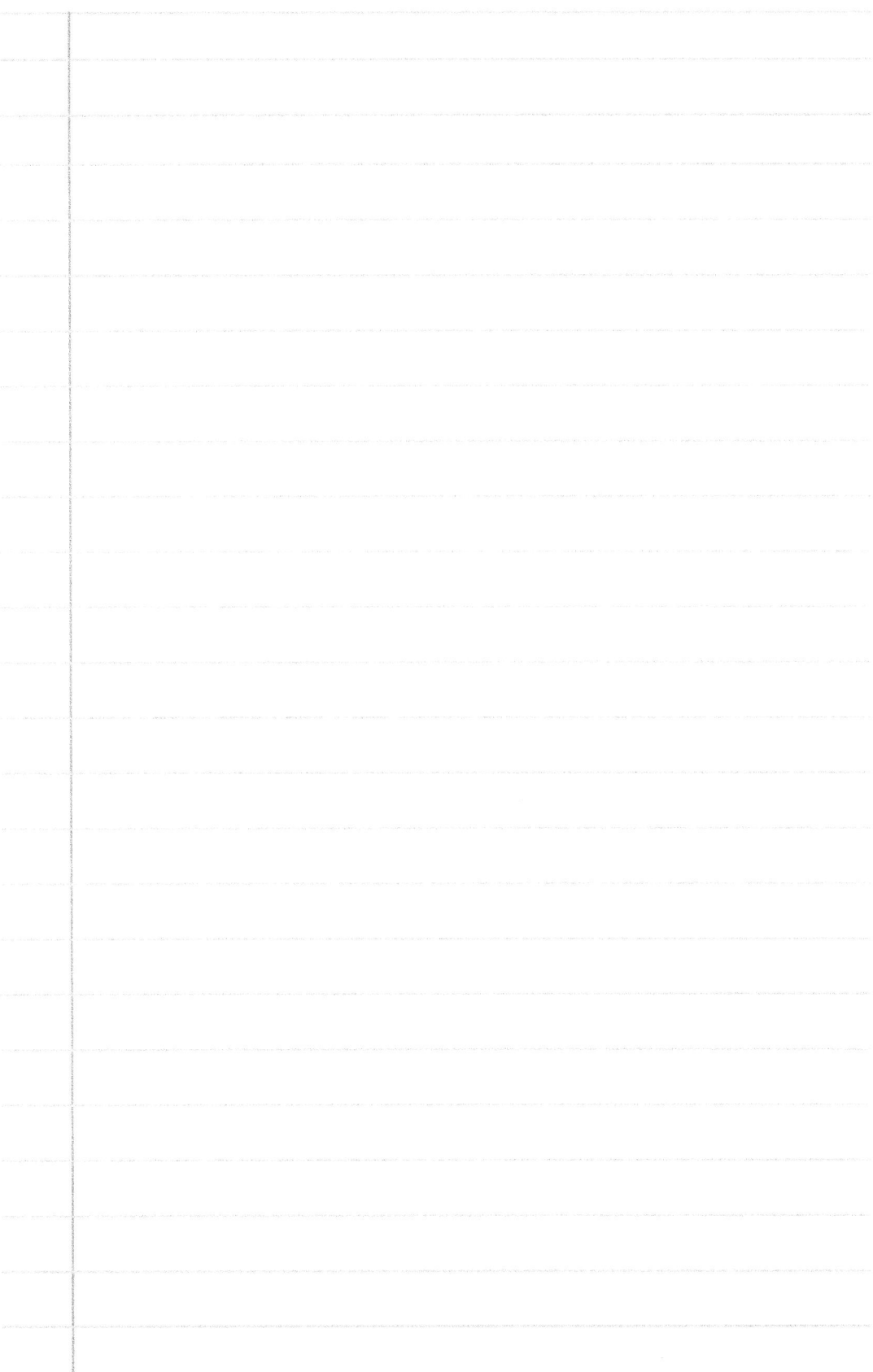

JULY

Week 1

Week 2

JULY

Week 3

Week 4

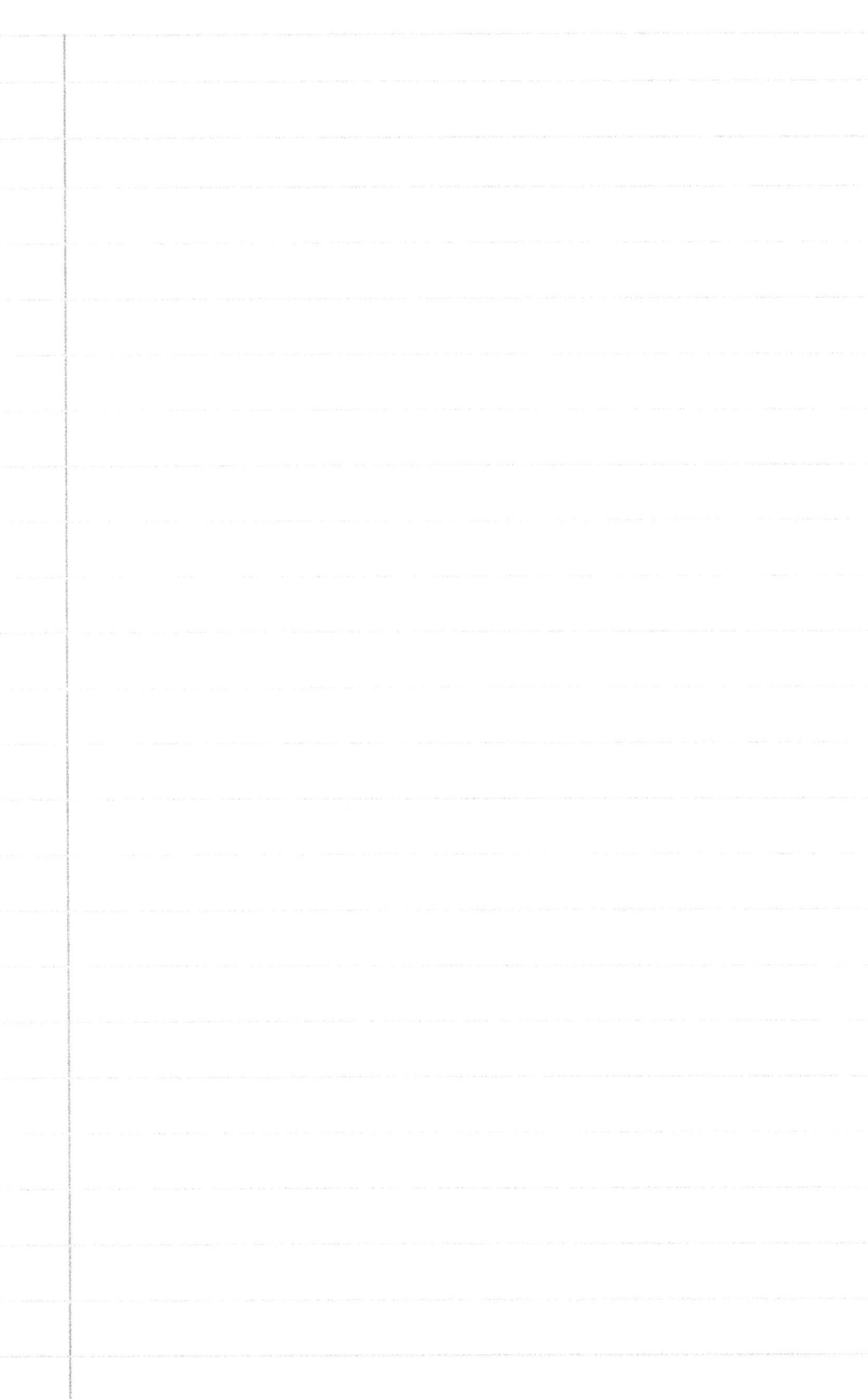

AUGUST

Week 1

Week 2

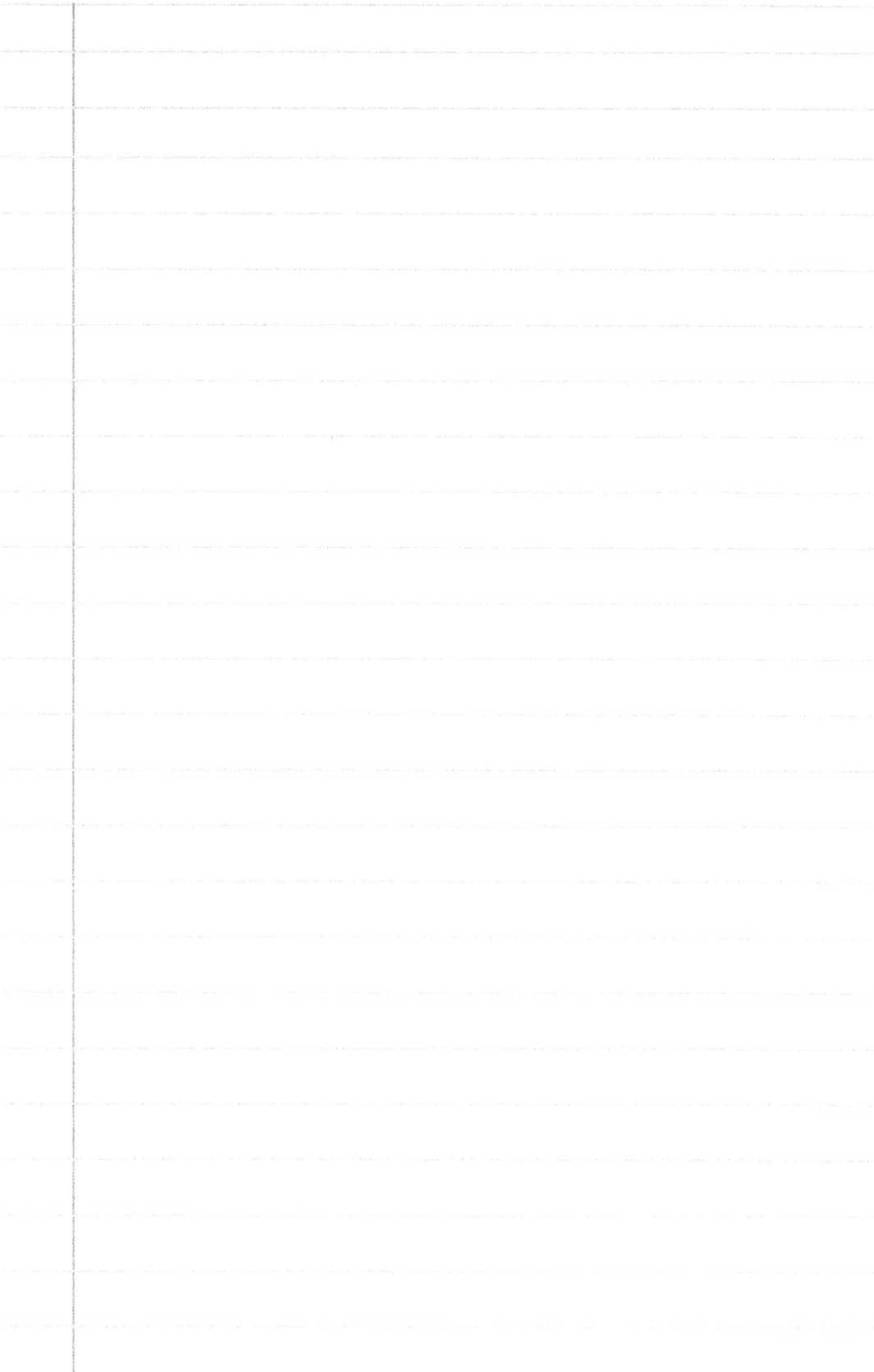

AUGUST

Week 3

Week 4

SEPTEMBER

Week 1

Week 2

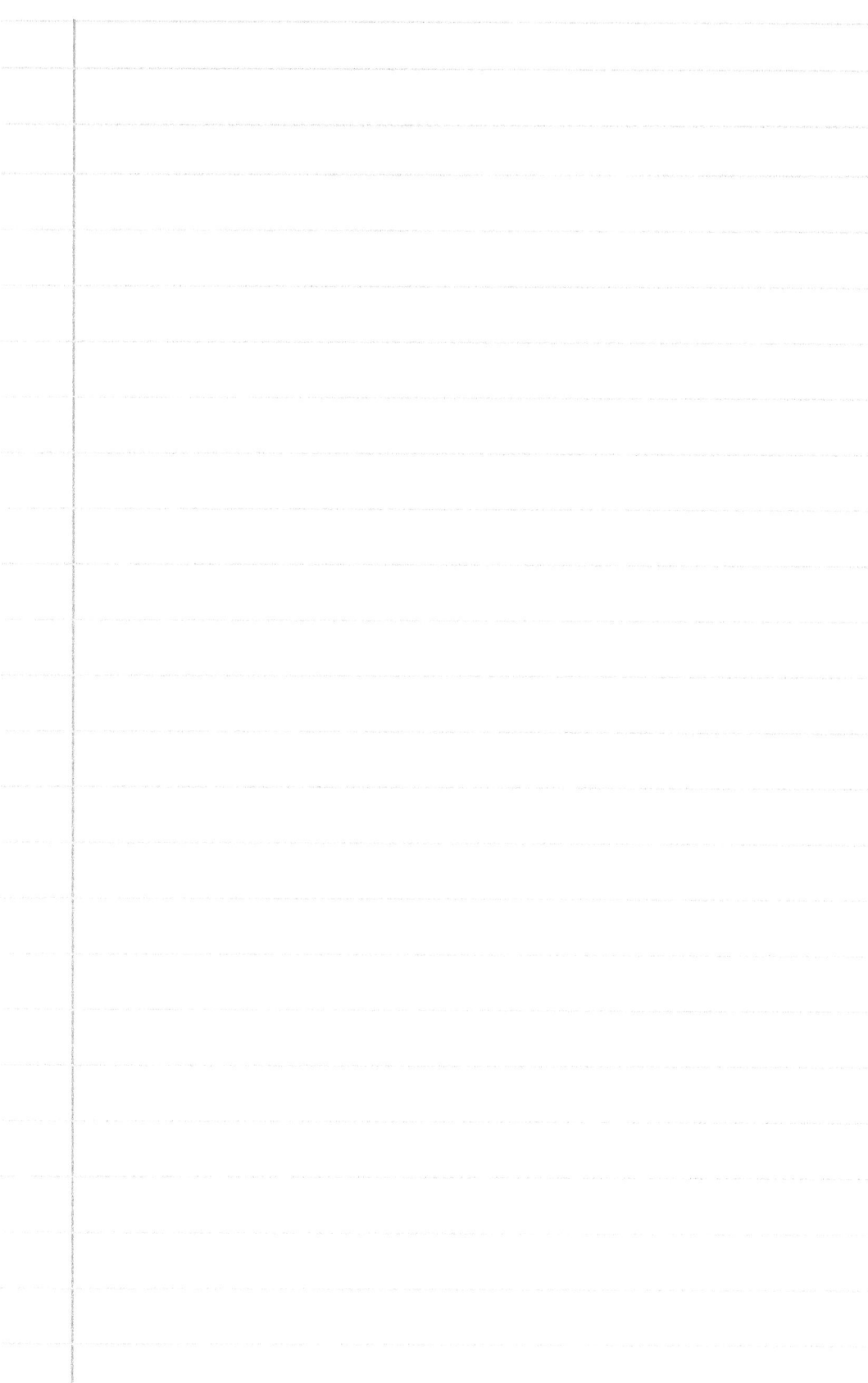

SEPTEMBER

Week 3

Week 4

OCTOBER

Week 1

Week 2

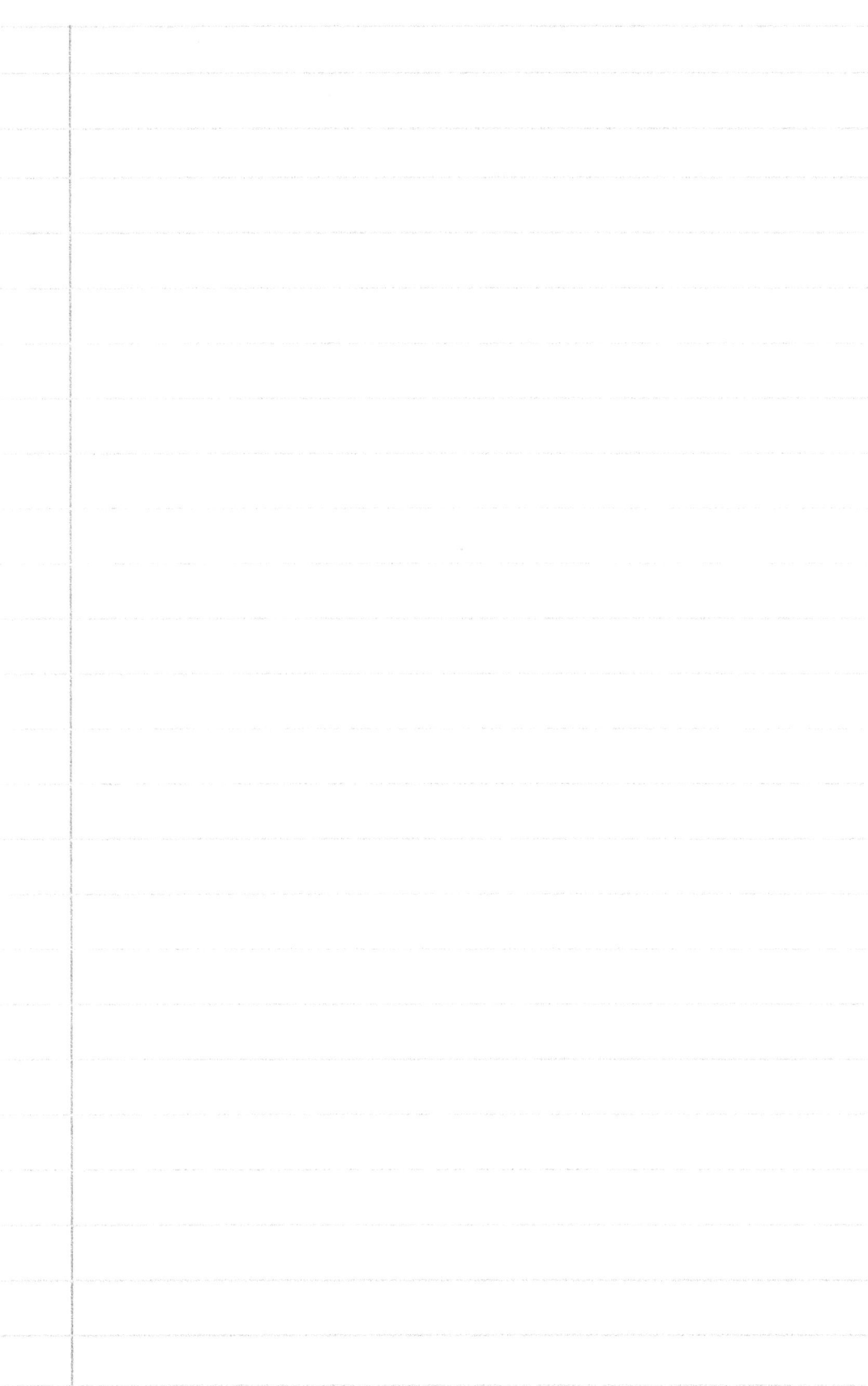

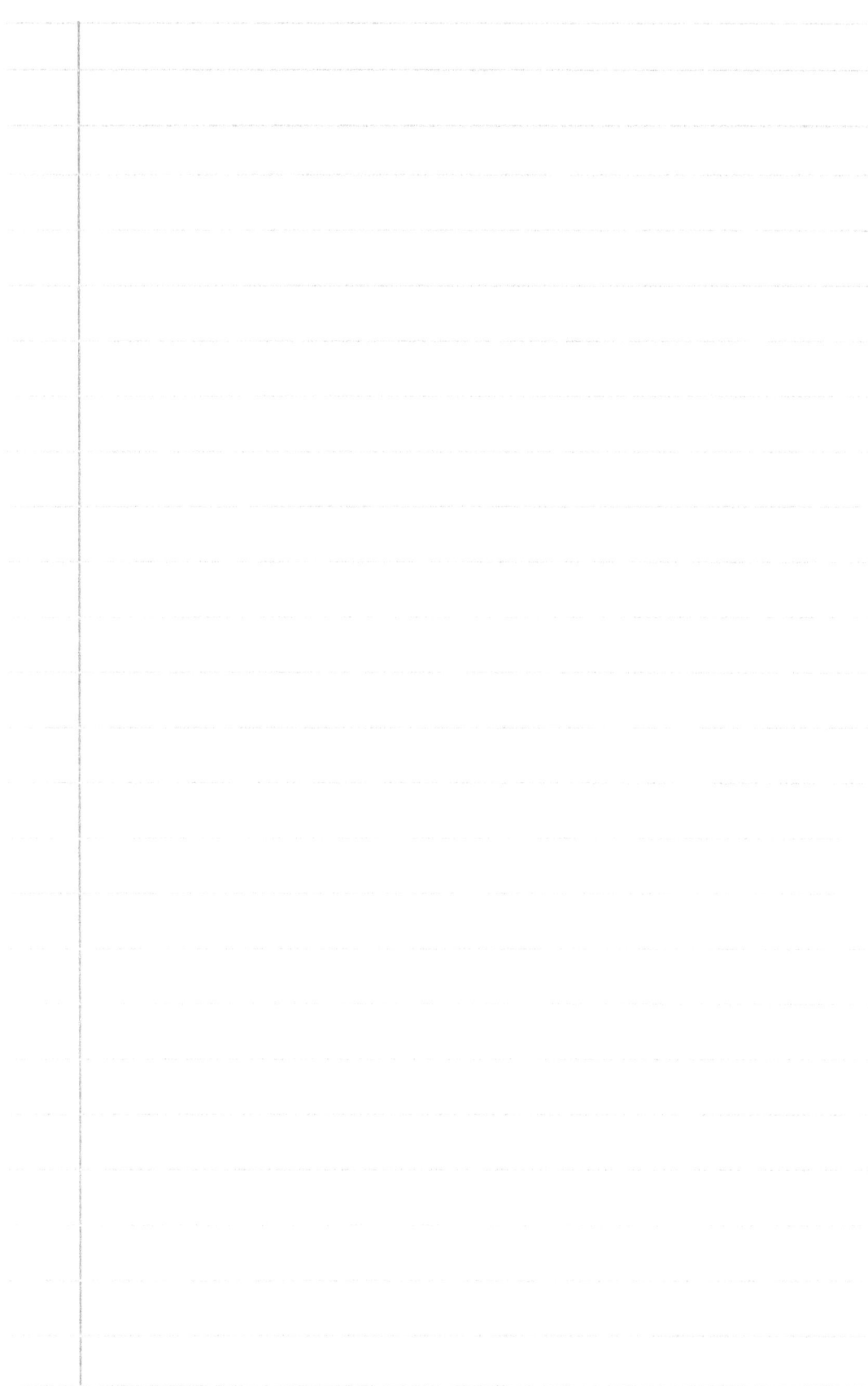

OCTOBER

Week 3

Week 4

NOVEMBER

Week 1

Week 2

NOVEMBER

Week 3

Week 4

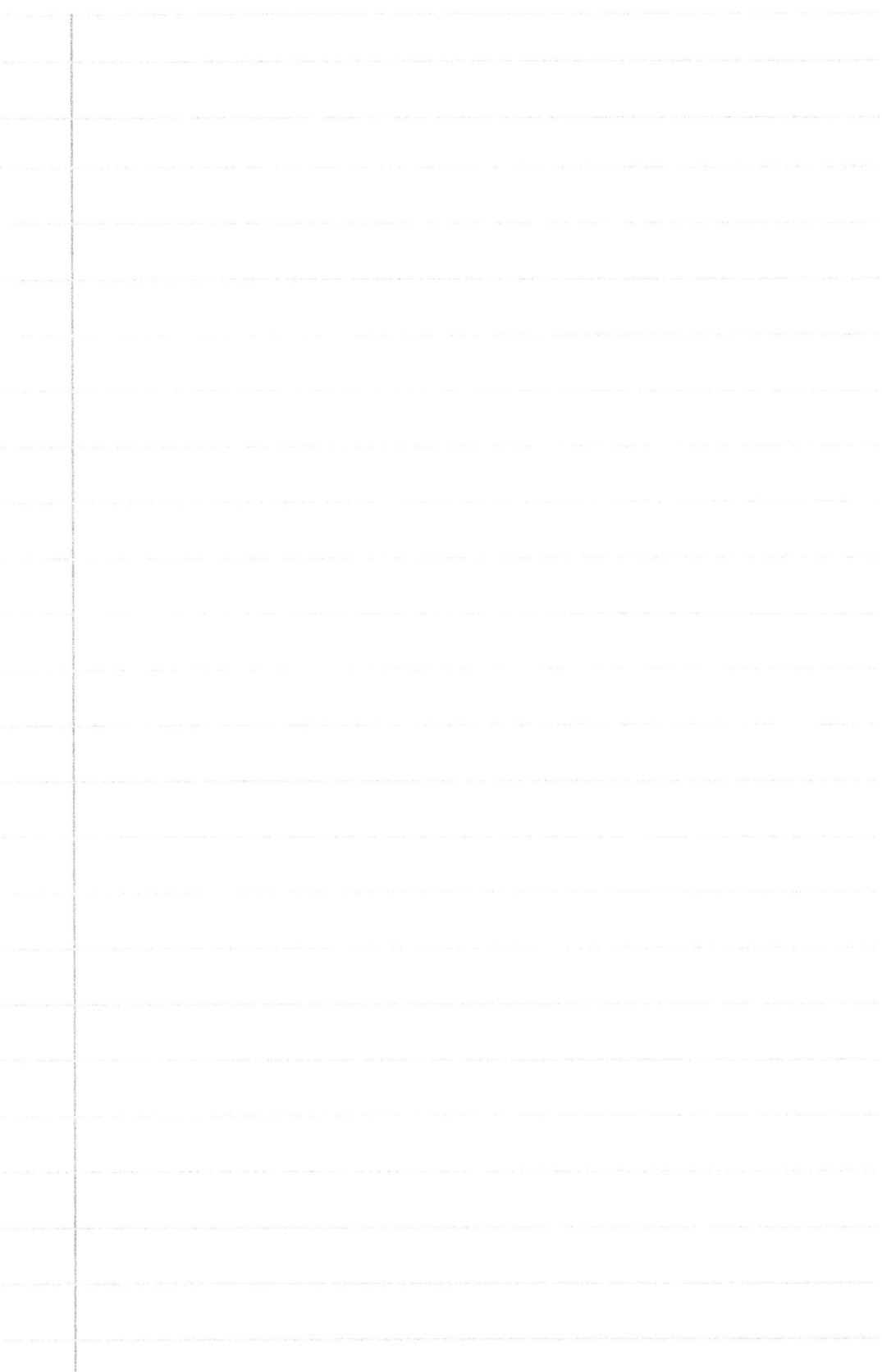

DECEMBER

Week 1

Week 2

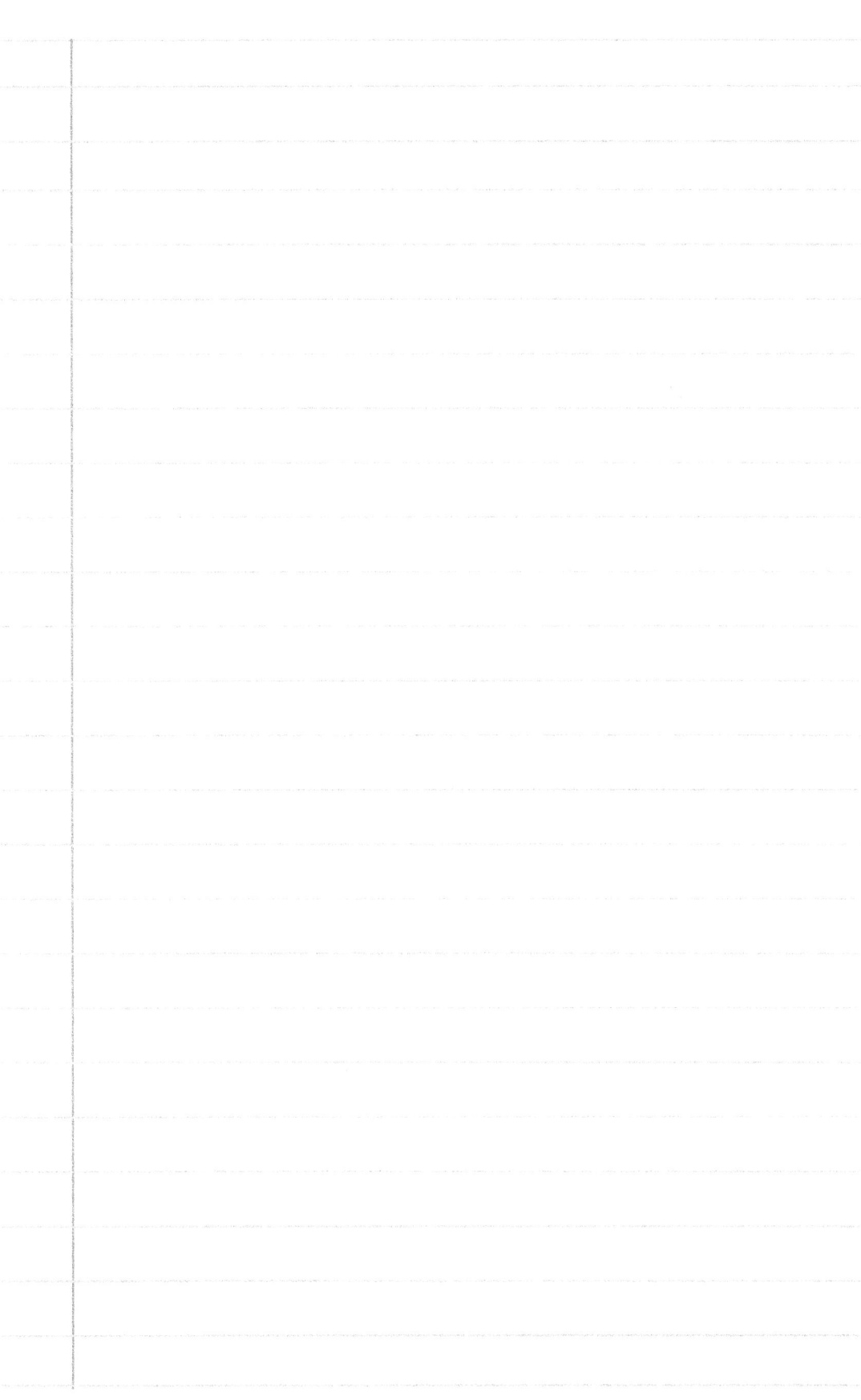

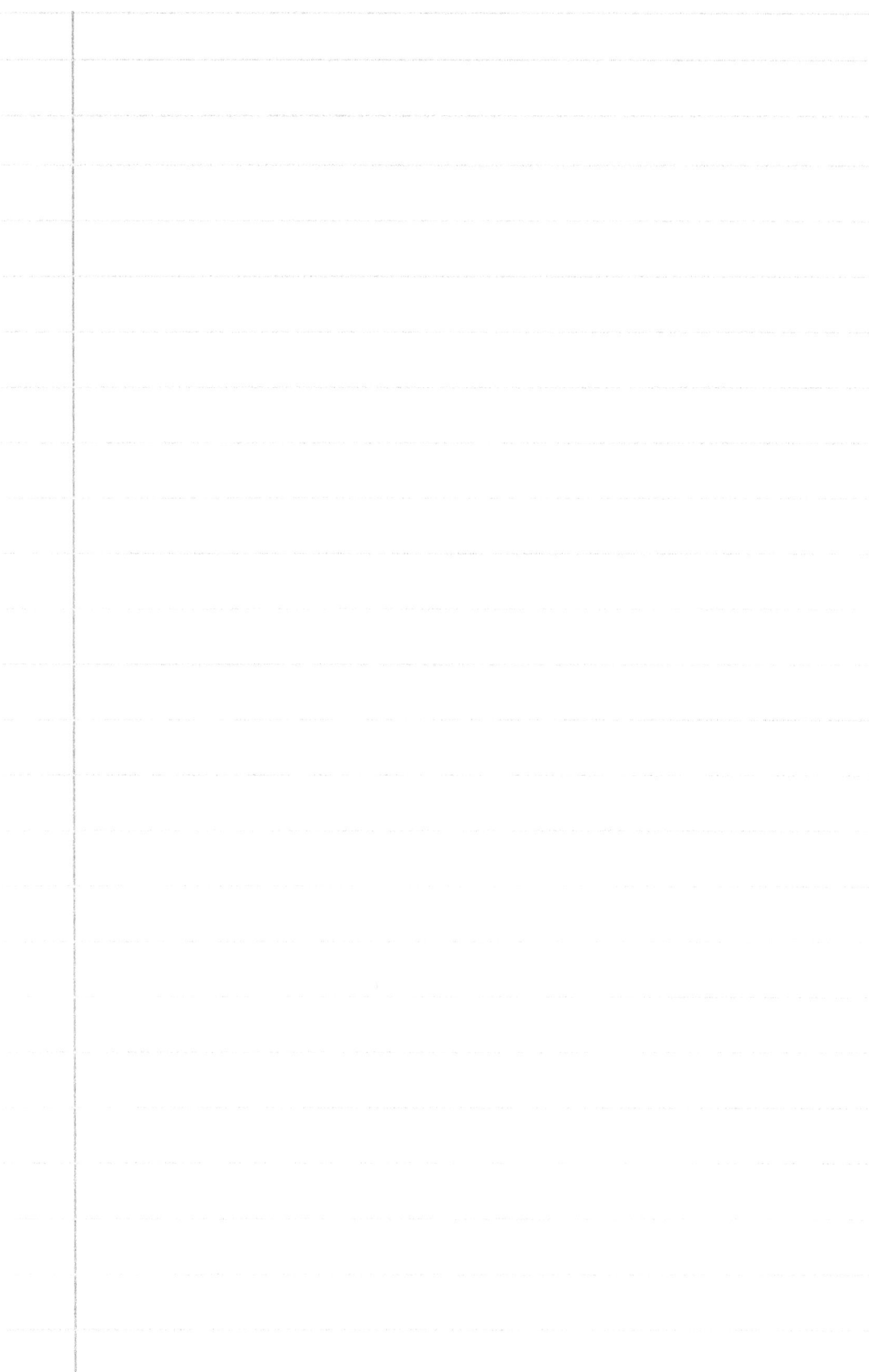

DECEMBER

Week 3

Week 4

Thanks for purchasing this book.
I would really appreciate it if you could review my book on Amazon. Reviews really help a new publisher like me get the word out and help reach other users.

www.ingramcontent.com/pod-product-compliance
Lightning Source LLC
Chambersburg PA
CBHW080608220526
45466CB00010B/3287